Fifth World
—A Poetic Journey

Fifth World
–A Poetic Journey

Creation Tales to Modern Musings

benn welch

FIFTH WORLD—A POETIC JOURNEY
CREATION TALES TO MODERN MUSINGS

Illustrations by Steven Olson
Photography by Bryan Wolff

iUniverse books may be ordered through booksellers or by contacting:

iUniverse
1663 Liberty Drive
Bloomington, IN 47403
www.iuniverse.com
1-800-Authors (1-800-288-4677)

ISBN: 978-1-4917-9205-6 (sc)
ISBN: 978-1-4917-9204-9 (e)

Library of Congress Control Number: 2016906751

Print information available on the last page.

iUniverse rev. date: 05/12/2016

For
STEVE
and
JAMES
JEANETTE
GREG

Do not be content with the stories of others.
Unfold your own myth.

- Rumi

Contents

Book of Laughter and Logic

Book of Memory's Gallery

Introduction

On this poetic journey some creation tales are retraced to see metaphoric truths that have always been there for the seeker. Throughout history many native peoples relied upon descriptive explanations, both simple and complex, of their existence. Growing up on Louisiana's gulf coast I was early aware of the Chitimacha, Houma, Coushatta, and Atakapa native tribes around me, and of my family's contacts with some of them. In *re ~viewing* some tales from indigenous peoples you'll find some observations from which to draw insight. ("Book of Creations")

Traversing Louisiana's Cajun bayou country will show a variety of life experience, as we look at the descendants of the refugees exiled in 1775 from *Acadie* in French Canada. This is my birthright, inheriting from this chronicle by both nature and nurture. Food and language are spiced and peppered from both native and immigrant cultures in a wonderful *repas a manger* (good food) and pervasive *patois* (dialect). ("Book of Memory's Gallery")

Sandwiched between these two cultural icons are modern musings about the "now" in which we find ourselves. Contemporary man finds an easier path of looking outward, setting life's course from this judgment. Looking inward, assessing the thoughts about what is seen, may be a healthier and more beneficial option. Along this journey, much like a genealogical chart of human nature, look at your experiences perhaps finding personal truths that may have been overlooked or forgotten. ("Book of the Seekers") Take the poetic journey where laughter acts as a medicinal, and look at the logic, the sensibleness, of life's experiences, ordinary and extraordinary, saddening and sublime. ("Book of Laughter and Logic")

On this rhythmical trek through the language of origins to modern musings, be the seeker you were meant to be and find inspiration to unfold your story, if only to yourself.

Book of Creations

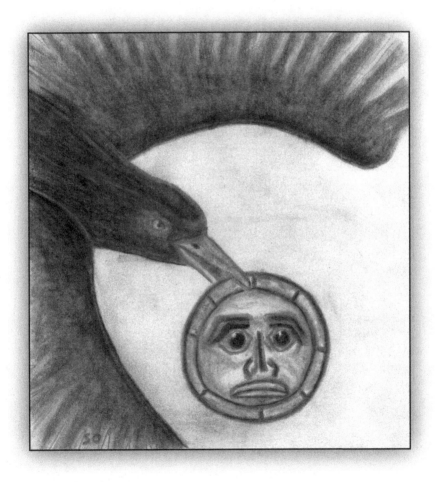

"Dark was conquered by Raven's flight . . ."

The Fifth World
A Maya Creation Tale

In This Beginning . . .

There was only infinite Sky above
and the waters of a vast Ocean below.
The space between was void, empty
except for voices thundering in echo.

For the gods were conversing, the wish
for creatures was their unending desire,
but with vapory Sky and watery Ocean
their creation would firm Earth require.

So the creators spoke into the mist
clearing the cloud-hovering Skies,
calling across the churning Ocean
for the drowned land to rise.

First World

For this new Earth they created animals
in forms and colors of great variety.
This new life was grandly expressed
but all the gods received was anxiety.

The plans were toward affinity
but all was a howl and a squawk.
What they desired was communion
with beings that would talk.

So the gods gave the noisy ones over
to this strident squabble, not understood.
This led to a different life as some
became their brothers' food.

Second World

A new attempt for a desirable being
was one molded of Earth's mud and clay.
It was susceptible to rain and moisture,
becoming featureless to the gods' dismay.

Though fragile, it had eyes, ears and speech,
but the words were of no value or worth.
The disheartened lords of creation
called the disfigured ones forth.

Tired of this grating idle chatter
and tired of mending rain-melted features,
they let them dissolve back to mud
and sought other sensible creatures.

Third World

In a third attempt the gods tried wood.
These looked human and had human speech.
Soon the gods saw these had no soul,
so knowing their creators was out of reach.

The gods decided to rid this no-soul world
of these creatures made of wood.
Jaguars and animals attacked many,
others were lost in rain and flood.

Some of the wooden people did escape
to deep forest and mountain places,
surviving as monkeys, losing speech
but mimicking human faces.

Fourth World
In a new quest the gods deliberate
possibilities for a new human plan.
From a paste of yellow and white corn grains,
an ancient goddess would mold a man.

These new humans pleased the gods
for they spoke to the gods with respect.
Seen as perfect men in all their ways,
the gods now feared their one neglect.

These had no world-conscious knowledge
thus lacking wisdom and reason,
so the gods breathed a mist into their eyes
to limit perfection and cloud their vision.

Fifth World

With man's journey on the ocean of time,
the gods are meeting in counsel again.
Poor-sighted humans put all in distress
and many call for a new human plan.

Amid numerous years with triumphs and failures,
there should come knowledge and insight.
With wisdom will these humans see it
and rise above their current plight?

Some humans are slaves to their fears.
To clear reason this fear makes them blind.
In primeval bias they proclaim the end,
time no more for mankind.

A New World

Excitement builds for a new world coming
with "unblinded" humans mirroring the divine.
The gods wait as the calendar counts,
giving man enlightenment time.

Are there earlier creations like "mud people"
with nonsense speech here again,
with marred or missing attributes
needing mending from conflicting rain?

Are there "wooden people" who look human,
have human speech but have no soul,
cannot recognize the creator but procreating,
bringing the Fifth World pain and woe?

The gods wait for wisdom-keepers to arise,
then will clear the clouded vision of mankind,
so creation sees the new perfect beings
that in the beginning was in the gods' mind.

Sometime in the Yesterdays
A First People Creation Tale

1.

In the yesterdays many counts ago,
Turtle arose from the deep of the Sea.
Covered in mud he appeared black
because all was hard to see.

All was dark with a dim light afar
peeking from the edge of Sky.
This was the time of only night
and many yesterdays went by.

Yesterday many counts past,
the mud dried on Turtle's shell,
curling from each muddy crease.
Turtle was pleased. All was well.

As Turtle floated the Great Sea,
he laughed at mud shapes that formed.
In this way creatures came to be,
making Turtle happy, not alarmed.

2.

Yesterday many counts past,
a Great Wind blew in a gentle storm,
bringing Breath from the edge of Sky
to enliven each mud-creature form.

These began to move around
greeting each other on Turtle's back.
With this movement and sound,
change came to those mud-black.

Yesterday with new ways to try,
the mud-ones grew as varied beings.
Some grew feathers and some grew hair,
others had legs, some had wings.

Some having feathers did not take wing.
Others had fur or just thick skin.
Most desired to dwell on Turtle land
but some loved the Sea and journeyed in.

3.

Yesterday sometime in the past,
creatures were curious of dark Sky.
On Turtle's back, a bleak view,
but at Sky's edge is light. Why?

Eagle was unable to investigate.
He flies high not a distance away.
Owl was too busy flying the dark.
Curious Raven flew far every day.

Raven, as trickster, was thinking fast.
With humans in mind he had a whim.
Since they were his favorite target,
this task could be done for them.

Humans labored in the darkness for food.
Unlike others their eyes could not adapt,
so Raven would fly as best he could
to find why Sky's light was trapped.

4.

In the yesterdays many counts back,
Raven asked, "Who will go with me?
If one follows the Turtle-back path,
I'll fly to Sky's edge to see."

Raccoon can't go because he is small.
Wolf can't go for he never travels alone.
Bear stood up looking fierce and tall,
"I'll go," he said, and he was gone.

Sometime then with Bear on the path,
Raven winged to the edge of the night.
At last he burst out of the black
and flew into the vivid light.

There, in light beyond Sky's edge,
Raven saw the source of the bright.
To the radiant jewel, called Sun, he flew
asking permission to borrow its light.

5.

In these yesterdays gone by,
Sun agreed to Raven's home flight
if Moon came along to traverse Sky,
for Moon borrowed Sun's light.

Happy to take Sun and Moon,
Raven soon grew tired in his flight.
Seeing a great lake he asked Moon
to wait there until Bear was in sight.

Yesterday as seen with new light,
Raven flew along with Sun's glare.
He motioned Bear waiting nearby
that Moon was now his care.

Raven pointed to Moon near water's edge
and Bear knew what to do,
but bright light hid Moon from sight
though Bear searched all the day through.

6.

In the yesterdays we can see
the mud-ones tarry in the dark and wait,
watching where Raven was last seen
and fearing what might be his fate.

While watching the edge of Sky,
expressing and debating their care
and thinking of Raven's brave deed,
they failed to see change everywhere.

In these days it happened at last.
Black mountains turned to purple cast,
the Great Sea and rivers azure blue,
and shades of green in trees and grass.

The sunflower a splash of yellow,
tree fruits of oranges and reds,
emergence of colors was subtly made,
while mud-creatures watched Sky's edge.

7.

In the yesterdays counts gone by,
the waiting mud-creatures became aware
of light replacing the enveloping black,
flashing varied colors everywhere.

Dark was conquered by Raven's flight
so far to the edge of the black,
returning with Sun in his beak
to mud-creatures on Turtle's back.

In the yesterday with Raven's flight,
the dark world flooded with light.
Mud-creatures no longer mud-black
were many-colored in a world quite bright.

As Raven flew across the lit sky,
mud-creatures rejoiced on Turtle's back,
until Raven tired of flying so high
carrying Sun to keep away the black.

8.

In the yesterdays many counts past,
tired Raven came down to the land.
Wearied of the toil Raven let Sun go,
but Sun stayed needing no hand.

Sun made the journey all on its own
but soon was very far away.
Falling to land o'er which it had shown
made this the mud-creatures first day.

In the yesterdays some counts back,
when Raven rested from his flight,
Bear was still searching for Moon
not noticing the drain of Sun's light.

Soon Sun needed a resting time
disappearing beyond Turtle's back,
leaving such a Sky of colors sublime,
who could remember the mantle of black?

9.

In the yesterdays many counts back,
the cloak of dark came to reclaim Sky.
Mud-ones were becoming mud-black.
For hero Raven they began to cry.

Raven wanted rest and needed food,
explaining to creatures now mud-black
there would again be light indeed,
for he would fly to bring Sun back.

In the yesterdays looking back,
Bear kept up his search for Moon.
Vowing to seek though sky was black,
Bear discovered it none too soon.

The shimmering Moon, as Raven said,
lay luminous in the lake's edge,
so Bear took Moon and was on his way.
For mud-creatures he kept his pledge.

10.

In the yesterdays many counts past,
with creatures in the first night's grip,
sun reappeared casting long shadows
so Raven was spared the tiring trip.

Raven's deed was a one-time flight
for Sun remembered the way back.
Each day newborn with Sun's glow
and each night like the days of black.

In the yesterdays of many days passed,
Bear traveled with Moon night and day.
That's why Moon's journey is longer
for Bear stopped to eat along the way.

Sometimes sideways, getting a bite,
Moon shines only a portion to view.
Sometime his back is to us at night
and Moon is hidden from view.

11.

In the yesterdays many counts gone by,
with Sun by day but resting at night,
the creatures were amazed at the night sky
with a bright orb changing shape and sight.

Raven said the night light was Moon,
not present where Sun did not go.
Its size was the same as Sun,
its light borrowed from Sun's glow.

In the yesterdays in a heroic try,
Bear arrived with the Moonbeam,
mud-creatures cheered as Bear went by
to deposit his charge in the stream.

They chanted for Bear to look up.
The night sky was gleaming clear,
and when Bear looked upward,
there was his Moon-friend dear.

12.

In our yesterdays a few counts ago,
Turtle-back creatures learned to see
how Raven's Sun kept a timely track,
so return of black was not to be.

Raven was given a place of esteem
in the stories on Turtle's back.
As trickster he still tried to jest
with those formerly mud-black.

In our yesterdays all could rely
on Moon to keep a known Sky track.
For Bear had walked Moon under Sky,
helping Raven carry light back.

Bear was praised for his heroic act
and like Raven given a place of favor.
Turtle-back creatures made a sure pact
to truly reward all courage and valor.

13.

Sometime in our yesterdays gone by,
they continued to pause and ponder
day's brilliant light and night's soft black,
nurturing them in awe and wonder.

They drank Sun's rays piercing the skies
or open-mouthed breathed the star-sight.
They never forgot Sky's once black shroud
and always rejoiced in Sun's light.

In this sometime a pledge was made:
"All mud-creatures true to this word be,
holding and seeing each creature dear,
alert and awake to all nature we see.

"Remembering our journey from Sea depth,
there on Turtle-back Mountains lifted,
and of Wind that brought us breath
while on the Sea, Turtle drifted."

Woman Who Fell from the Sky
A First Peoples Creation Tale

Once there was only water
covering Earth end to end.
Here lived one called Otter
and one, Beaver, his friend.

Other water animals were there
and among them feathered friends
like Duck and Goose, a pair
flying high, soaring the winds.

People were not here to be seen,
for they lived beyond Sun's glow
in the Sky-world, a place between
the Creator and Water-world below.

Then a strange thing happened one day.
Was it Star-pieces that fell?
Beaver and Otter ceased water-play
for this was news to tell.

The feathered friends were off in flight
but heard the call of Beaver and Otter.
They were puzzled by this sight
of Star-pieces falling to the water.

The water friends watched the pieces fall
and sink beside them in the water,
but the pieces were not bright at all.
Not from the Stars, believed Otter.

Duck and Goose flew higher again
to search an answer to the riddle
of this so-called Star-piece rain,
so they flew to the Star-rain middle.

A bright object came in sight
and it seemed to twinkle like a Star.
They almost stopped in their flight.
It was falling, but not a star.

Then happened a most startling thing.
They must hurry to tell Beaver and Otter
what they've seen, flying wing to wing.
From Sky-world, Woman falls to the water.

Duck and Goose flew down to the water
to tell water-friends this surprising news.
But what a discovery! Beaver and Otter
have totally different views.

Fear-filled were Beaver and Otter
watching Sky-Woman's fall downward,
for they were seeing it reflected in the water,
too frightened to look upward.

From above Duck and Goose call
downward to Beaver and Otter
with news of the woman's fall
in the Star-rain over the water.

With eyes on the reflecting water,
they said the woman was very near.
Up from the underworld, shouted Otter,
and believing this brought great fear.

Some insisted she was from Star-rain,
and agreed with Duck and Goose,
who then flew upward again,
leaving others to their limited views.

The dark pieces of stars stopped falling
as Sky-Woman was seen by the two.
Aye! Aye! The Sky-Woman was calling
when Duck and Goose came into view.

The brave ones flew to her side
and with overlapping wings to bear her,
gave the Sky-Woman a feathery ride,
protecting her from the dark water.

Gently they descended to Beaver and Otter,
whose gaze was now uplifted.
Seeing Duck and Goose in the mirrored water,
they realized their view was restricted.

With the Sky-Woman what should be done?
There were no old tales of such things.
They would go to Great Turtle, a wise one,
to show Woman in the basket of wings.

In haste off swam Beaver and Otter
as Feathered Friends flew along.
They found Great Turtle afloat in the water.
As Master his knowledge is strong.

Great Turtle, a sage, conscious of all,
waited for Beaver and Otter.
He had seen Woman from Sky-world fall
and Star-pieces drift to the water.

When the excited water-animals arrive,
he said she could be placed on his back,
but first they must downward dive
with no fear of the deep watery black.

Down in the depth of watery cold
they would find Star-pieces that fell.
This earth they'd scoop up, being bold,
and bring it back to cover his shell.

So Muskrat joined Beaver and Otter
and water-animals who were brave,
diving to the depths in unknown water,
trusting the words Great Turtle gave.

Taking the biggest of breaths
with one intention and purpose:
dive to the deepest of depths
bringing magic earth to the surface.

Depositing their diggings on Turtle's back,
they journeyed, to the underwater cold
for in bravery there was no lack.
Then feathery wings did gently unfold.

Sky-Woman slid from the basket of wings,
planting her feet on the earth-covered shell
bringing wonder to all the water beings,
but Great Turtle had more to tell.

Sky-Woman listened to what must be done,
for all needed to understand.
If the woman danced, following the Sun,
all the beings could share the land.

Though Great Turtle was large,
how could all share this new land?
Sky-Woman took up her charge
and danced Sun-wise as planned.

Aye! And a great happening came about,
for Turtle's back began to grow.
All the water-animals gave a shout,
and joined the dance in Sun's glow.

As she danced Turtle's back grew,
and grew into a big island expanse
with hills and valleys and mountains in view,
growing as long as Sky-Woman danced.

Finally Sky-Woman could dance no more,
and Turtle Island ceased to expand.
Many of the water-animals stayed ashore
after dancing in the new land.

This is how First People came to dwell,
how they and the animals share the lands,
how the land hugs Great Turtle's shell
and the magic of the Sun-wise dance.

And the story continues,
there is more to tell
of twin grandchildren
of Sky-Woman-Who-Fell.

One was selfish and cruel
and one brave and bold,
but that's another tale,
another time to be told.

The Song of the Gods
A Genesis Story

In this beginning the gods begin,
Begin to contemplate.
Their thought, where the abyss reigns,
A garden to originate.

But this thought needed a form,
The void needed a fill,
And out of the primal storm
A new earth to reveal.

So into the foggy strand
Where wind and wave held sway,
Came a voice like an unseen hand,
As in this beginning the gods say,

"Let us pull back the darkness
And birth a new day.
Let us push back the seas
And dry out Pangaea.

"Let us night-light the moon
And star-light the night.
Let us wind up the sun-clock
And space-spread its light."

As the gods' words took form,
The great void was filled,
And day and night were born,
Morn and eventide revealed.

Here it was then,
Father-Mother-Spirit create.
Thought became word when
The gods said, "Let us make."

Canto I

The Great Father spoke,
The Great Mother answered
And the Great Spirit gave breath.

1.

The Great Father spoke,
"Let there be grass and flowers and trees."

The Great Mother answered
In phenomenal degrees
With dark greens and light greens
And all greens between
And tiniest of plants
And trees so giant
And flowers with colors
From the rainbow palette
And a halo of fragrance
From the Mother's own breath,

And more, yes much more!

When presenting all She'd conceived,
The wind came in a whispered caress
As Great Spirit did upon them breathe
And the new Earth was well-dressed.

2.

The Great Father spoke,
"Let the no-legs be."

The Great Mother answered
In extraordinary glee
With great whales and goldfish
And giant squid and jellyfish
And monk seals and angelfish
sun perch and starfish
And pearl-making clams
Eels with electricity
Tail-shrinking tadpoles . . .
Oops! Are those legs we see?

And more, yes much more!

When presenting all She'd conceived,
The wind o'er waters rippled
As the Great Spirit did breathe
And Earth's waters were filled.

3.

The Great Father spoke,
"Let the feathered ones be."

The Great Mother answered
So phenomenally
With ostrich and oriole
And hummingbird and horned owl
And falcon and flamingo
A goldfinch and guinea fowl
And parrots that talk
And weaver birds that weave
A penguin . . . underwater?
How do they breathe?

And more, yes much more!

And when presenting all She'd conceived,
Over these new feathered beings
Wind of Great Spirit did breathe
And Earth's air filled of wings.

4.

The Great Father spoke,
"Let the four-legged appear."

The Great Mother answered
Most marvelously here
With lambs and lions
And aardvark and bear
And tigers and deer
A zebra and hare
And platypus and pack rat
And great apes and lynx
A beaver and . . . a bat!
Four feet and wings!

And more, yes much more!

And when presenting all She'd conceived,
Over each of reptile and beast
The wind of Great Spirit did breathe
And the Earth filled with feet.

Canto II

And the gods said,
"It is good, good,
And very good."

1.

The gods walked in this garden
In the cool of the day,
And the gods talked with creation
Of all that was made.

The gods listened to the music
That was heard garden-wide,
And the gods signaled an agreement
With smiles universe-wide.

2.

The mountains stood guardian
Of the great forests below,
And green mantles reached upward
Through clouds, rain, and snow.

The wind whistled through leaves,
Hummed 'round mountain towers,
And rainbows bowed in agreement
To follow the valley showers.

3.

The great Sun with warmth-light
Is always and clock-like the same,
And the moon always changing,
Playing some celestial game.

It's hide-and-seek in midday,
Not always there at night,
And the stars twinkle in agreement
Of the creators' might.

4.

The waters sang their song,
Brooks babbled like brooks,
And rivers wriggled over continents
In bends and turns and crooks.

Thunder-rolls and lightning-bolts
Played out grand theaters,
And raindrops applauded
The words of the creators.

5.

The trees bowed low
Gifting their treasures as fruits,
And for the health of the planet
Sharing leaves, bark, and roots.

The grasses grew greener,
Flowery blooms unfurled,
And butterflies air-danced accord
With the creators' world.

6.

The birds sang soprano,
Bullfrogs sang bass,
And cicadas hummed along
As crickets played their legs.

But coyotes are still trying
And donkeys are another case.
Still, the voices of agreement
Did fill every space.

Canto III

1.

The symphony had been chosen
And the soloists perfected,
The choir gloriously robed
And the orchestra selected.

In beauty and grace
Creation's music flowed.
Look who is directing
And who has composed.

2.

But something is missing,
What can it be?
Creation is magnificent.
We hear it, feel it and see.

The laws are in motion
To guide and provide,
Equal to all and true
The universe wide.

3.

So the Great Father drew inward
This question to solve.
As the Great Father thought,
A new word evolved.

And the Great Mother smiled,
Held open her hands
And the Great Spirit moved
To draw in a great breath.

4.

And the Great Father thought,
Let us make . . .
And the Great Mother thought,
Let us make . . .

And the Great Spirit thought,
Let us make . . .
And the gods said,
"Let us . . . sing." Sing?

5.

From the greatest impression
In the Great Father's mind
Came the perfect expression
Like a melody divine.

The Great Mother accepted this
That the Great Father expressed,
And the Great Mother bowed low,
Earth's clay to caress.

6.

The Mother's hand measured
And kneaded with care,
Leaving her impressions
Stamped here and there.

From the brown silt of riverbanks
And the sands of the sea,
And from the red earth of sunsets
Came the new form to be.

7.

From the dust of the stars
And rainbow pieces,
And moss from the trees
And sweet-scented breezes,

A little seawater spittle
And dewdrops of Eden,
She presented to creation
A divine composition.

8.

Its innermost heart
Came from the gods' song,
And from the best of nature
Came its sinew and bone.

This new man of Eden,
Perfect in all ways,
Needed the breath of life
To join creation's praise.

9.

Then the Great Spirit hovered
O'er this that was new,
And face to face breathed
Its own breath to imbue,

And all creation awed
At such act of grace
As life-breath emerged
From Spirit's embrace.

10.

So the gods made this song
In its own image,
Its very own heart,
And with its breath,

And all creation bowed
As the gods had done
To bend to the dust
To make this one;

11.

To mold it and hold it
And give it this life,
To impart its nature,
Its spirit and mind.

Creation still awes
Of this marvelous thing
That gives the gods a voice
And lets the gods sing.

12.

The gods sing everywhere,
Any tongue, any tempo.
Its always spontaneous,
No need for libretto.

The music is of our desire
And our own choosing.
The title of this song
Is simply, *Be ~ing.*

13.

As it was in the beginning,
So it is even now,
For the gods still sing
And their children know how.

We are that song
Brought to wondrous being,
So give the gods a voice
And let the gods sing.

Reprise

The Great Father speaks,
The Great Mother creates,
And the Great Spirit gives breath.

And the gods say,
"It is good, good,
And very good."

Book of the Seekers

"The journey may resemble a maze . . ."

A Theological Maze

The Buddha once was Hindu.
Jesus was a Jew.
Abraham was Moses' ancestor
And Muhammad's, too.

1.

The Buddha once was Hindu.
This religious creed, the first known,
Formed along the River Indus
As oral traditions have shown.

Gautama was his given name,
Born in a cradle of wealth,
Guarded by walls and distractions
Never to view death or ill health.

Once he saw outside these walls
He abdicated this privileged station
Vowing to search for meaning in life,
To become one with all creation.

A false road was one of physical denial
And when starved nigh to death drifting,
Came a youth touching milk to his lips,
Reviving his body, his spirit lifting.

He then began to teach disciples
The Middle Way, a centered stance
Lived not in total physical denial
Nor in abandon to extravagance.

Sitting in silence beneath the fig tree,
Gautama's thoughts and contemplation
Led him into that seeker's state
Of insight through meditation.

There it happened to this quester,
Brought to a place of universal seeing.
Gautama reached the Buddha state
As one with Unmanifest Being.

2.

Abram once was Chaldean
Who worshiped the moon and sun.
He lived in lower Mesopotamia
Where mythical Eden rivers run.

From living in the Fertile Crescent
Abram moved to the Mediterranean Sea.
He changed his name to Abraham
And also changed his theology.

No longer gave he adoration to things
Like fire and water, moon and sun,
But rather looked at the Source of all
As anthropomorphic - a great Someone.

Ishmael was Abraham's son, firstborn,
Child of Hagar, the Egyptian maid.
Wife Sarah mothered him as her own,
For she was barren and much aged.

Then Sarah bore a son, naming him Isaac.
Wanting this son to be inheritor alone
She quoted divine oath sending Ishmael away
Though for years he was loved as her own.

Exiled to the harsh desert was the youth
With his mother, the handmaid.
Theology had made their plight sure death
But the Someone provided food and shade.

Seems the Someone doesn't ask theologically
Who's Sarah's child or who's of the handmaid.
The Someone sends the sun and rain to all.
In sustenance, the Someone's hand is not stayed.

3.

Moses once was an Egyptian prince
For the Pharaoh's daughter heard an infant's cry
And found baby Moses afloat in the Nile,
His Hebrew sister watching nearby.

To the Pharaonic palace Princess brought Moses.
His sister true offered to nurture the boy,
caring for him daily through many years.
Was teaching him theology a covert employ?

As a royal the youth got instruction
In religion from priests and writing from scribes.
Did he hear of Akhenaten and his one-god religion?
Did it sound like the one his sister describes?

When this nursemaid told of Abraham's god,
And the state religion showed a different aspect,
Could young Moses choose of the two ideas
Some to acquire and some to reject?

Perhaps the central point of this conjecture
Is to realize what many see as gods diffuse
Are the many faces and guises of the One,
Seen from the many postures we observers use.

Soon he makes of the two worlds a choice,
Is disowned by the royals, and estranged.
Joining the Bedouin in Arabia's desert,
Seems his theology becomes rearranged.

With a historical genesis from Egypt's books,
And a new law list, 'Thou shalt not',
That comes not from Abraham's god, Elohim,
But from Yahweh, the new Fire Mountain god.

Still Moses invokes the god of Abraham
While writing down the tribe's genealogy,
And visits the thundering mountain of Yahweh
To write more briefs on this hybrid theology.

4.

Born the son of a carpenter,
Learning the trade as he grew,
Building a compassionate philosophy,
Jesus was a Jew.

Mother Mary had been visited
By the Archangel Gabriel
And told of this special child-to-be
Whom prophets called Immanuel.

"God with us" was the meaning
And from an early age
The child showed great intellect,
Debating with the wisdom of a sage.

When he spoke healing to the sick
And brought the self-righteous to censure,
The commoner called him Teacher
While the religious raged displeasure.

He was not seen for several years
And it was said he was in the desert alone.
It's also said he journeyed to India
Where references to him are shown.

Whatever its source his message was heard.
His philosophy was love without condition.
Calling for peacemakers and the pure of heart,
It needed no religious rendition.

But religiosity was too engrained.
It is said he was executed, no escape to be.
His philosophy did not the religious change
But survives in a varied theology.

5.

Muhammad was near to being an orphan
For before he was born, his father died.
His name was Abdullah, living in Mecca,
Home of the Hashim clan, Quraish tribe.

From Abraham's firstborn, Ishmael,
The tribe said the lineage had come.
The patriarch brought Ishmael and mother here
To make it their new home.

Their tent was pitched near Kaaba,
From earliest times a religious shrine.
In respect to a divine directive
Abraham lived here part-time.

The shrine's most valued artifact
Was the Black Stone. A meteorite?
Father and son rebuilt the sacred house
And their progeny guarded the holy site.

By the time of Muhammad's birth
A city around Kaaba had grown.
Mecca, its name, became a caravan stop
For most cultures and creeds then known.

With the caravans to this cosmopolis,
Hundreds of idols and gods came.
A bustling economy built around them
But drunkenness and idolatry became its fame.

To a cave on the Mount of Light
Muhammad retreated to meditate.
There the angel Gabriel appeared
To help him read though illiterate.

His original creed of basic laws of justice
Replaced Arab, Jewish, and Christian tribal laws
With a rule all inclusive of class, color, and creed,
Making peaceful coexistence its just cause.

6.

Of this grid-like theological maze,
The path has been tread through the ages,
Meandering its twists and turns and stops,
Inspired and exhorted by its Guides and Sages.

Each in turn presenting a differing vista
With a guide of a different name.
The words and cultures may rearrange
But the path remains the same.

The journey may resemble a maze
When your corridor seems at its end.
Think of this plight more as a puzzle,
And find the piece that fits in.

These Guides looked over the constrictive walls
Of this man-made theological maze,
And pulled into the general view
Some insights from philosophical haze.

Some glean insight from an older view.
Some espouse one that seems totally new.
Some bring us back to original thought.
Some make a hybrid of two.

All eventually looked within themselves,
Not in verdict, but with resolve,
And saw the function of this life
Is letting human spirit evolve.

The Quest

1.
When asked of life,
Where is god?
I listened.
Life spoke no word,

And
When asked of god,
What is life?
I listened.
Nothing was heard.

2.
When asked of the cosmos,
What of our genesis?
I listened.
No cosmic voice was heard,

And
When asked of nature,
How and why is this?
I listened.
Nature uttered no word.

3.
When asked of mankind,
What of the divine?
I deafened
From a torrent of words,

And
When asked of those words,
Show me the divine?
I waited.
Little seen, more words.

4.

When asked of myself,

Where is hope?

I waited and heard,

But the chatter was unintelligible,

And

When asked of hope,

Who is this self?

I stopped!

The words were barely audible.

5.

Halting in this asking,

Be silent and still,

I said.

Could no answer be mine?

And
Then came the small voice within.
It's here, it's here,
It whispered,
It's been here all the time.

6.
It's Life. It's Nature. It's Cosmos.
It's all the Divine, It said.
I knew!
But it was a knowing unheard.

So
Questing no more,
I saw It's all God.
I knew!
That's the unspoken word.

The Lost Book

I

A book was lying in the canyon road
between the narrow contrary lanes, lost.
A sizable volume there for several days
with all its words traffic-tossed.

No place to stop for its rescue
so the pages flutter to and fro,
hectic traffic fingering its leaves
as if searching for a telling quote.

Tibetans hang their entreaties as flags
and unseen winds carry the messages off.
What subject rides the breezes here,
pious or profane that's sent aloft?

Words are a way thoughts express,
and written, a way to pass them on,
whether inked on wet papyrus
or chiseled in faceted stone.

To look at diverse and varied marks
with standard order and fixed traits,
and to understand their hidden meaning
is an amazing feat of the human race.

II

Like the book lying in harried traffic
and none able its words to assess,
one thinks of our illiterate ancestors
replicating this word-thought process.

Perhaps around the collective fires
the fascinating myth-story was shown,
or absorbed at the feet of aging elders,
or covert kept for the privileged alone.

Once there was no written word
or even a spoken word known.
Then, before there were words,
were thoughts a process unknown?

If known, how this thought transfer?
Was it shared in a mutual glance?
Were they pictured on a cave wall,
told by hand-signs or in a dance?

Giving no slight to the ancestors
dwelling in a sea of sounds, though near-mute
they perceived a near-silent communication
that traveled sensory paths most acute.

III

But there's the book on this "Samaritan" road
where hundreds pass it daily, a seeming crime.
Its theme and value to us unknown
but its author labored hours or a lifetime.

Recall history's book-burners and censors
afraid one would grasp a word and think.
Fearing this word-thought could be evil-inspired,
tried they did to control the ink.

Intrinsically veiled within great words written
are reflections of reason and intention,
mutely waiting for the earnest pursuer
to welcome thought in high-sensory attention.

Shocking then to pass this inspiring spot
and miss the verbose fluttering pages.
The now public book had near vanished
with its wind sown mystery messages.

All that was dejectedly noticeable now
were a few lacerate leaflets, still unread,
for censoring autos had tread its white pages
leaving sullied fragments with no linking thread.

There is a Door

There is a Door, not hidden at all,
There, to a Great Room with naught to hide.
There is no guard, except our dreams.
There is no key.
There is a keyhole.
    What's inside?

What stories we've heard of the hidden!
What musings the imagination supplies!
What fable or foible! What dictum! What dream!
What is fact?
What is fiction?
    Whose reasoning applies?

Whose legend can deliver its treasure?
Whose mystery has any evidence shown?
Whose lengthy debate? Whose ethereal dream?
Whose code?
Whose canon?
    Can answers be known?

Can the Door be forced? It seems not.
Can the walls be scaled or felled to ground?
Can knowing the truth be a possible dream?
Can we ignore it?
Can you?
  Is there a key to be found?

Is the key a magic number or a mystery word?
Is there a hidden cipher or a mystical rhyme?
Is it possible to find it in a dream?
Is it here?
Is it there?
  Will we find it in time?

Will we know it when we see it?
Will the seeker find what's sought?
Will it appear in life or in a dream?
Will it be euphoric?
Will we fear?
  Do we quest for naught?

Do we ask the wrong question?

Do we look in the right direction?

Do the clues brazenly surface in our dreams?

Do we see it?

Do we look?

    Why no detection?

Why do treasures seem always hidden?

Why should such a profound search be?

Why does the seeking seem as a dream?

Why dream?

Why not?

    When will we be free?

When will this freedom arrive?

When will we cease this endless quest?

When will it end, or is the end a dream?

When, this ceasing?

When, this release?

    We abruptly stop, are still, and rest.

We are forever asking what and why and where.
We ask when and how and so much more.
We weaken our vision living in another's dream.
We awaken.
We see it there.
> It's the Door!

It's before us. We kneel. We want to bow.
It's a shrine of which we've heard orations.
It's observed. It's not just a dream.
It's revered.
It's honored.
> We've done oblations.

We've garnered mysteries surrounding the portal.
We've substituted custom for truth's pure sinew.
We've dictated divine directives and ascribed an
> aberrant dream.

We've failed.
We've repented.
> Shall we thus continue?

Shall we canonize the self-appointed doorkeepers?
Shall we acquiesce to theory, knowing we lose?
Shall we opt for sobriety and heed our dreams?
Shall we hope?
Shall we fear?
    We must choose.

We sort through the ecclesiastical clutter.
We see what it portends - the Great Room of lore.
We remember the keyhole. We recall our dreams.
We laugh.
We cry.
    Our emotions soar.

Our sight was so subtly blinded before.
Our stumbling about was a path we treasured.
Our lives were lived in a derelict's dream.
Our choice?
Our perspective?
    By whose philosophy measured?

By a petty premise we were pabulum fed.

By prescribed ritual we made sacred pretense.

By following and not thinking we tread a false
   dream.

By whose fault?

By theirs?

   Maybe it's <u>S</u>elf-<u>I</u>nflicted <u>N</u>onsense.

Maybe it is simple nonsense and not mortal sin.

Maybe it is self-inflicted and not the other's cause.

Maybe it is time we abandon their dreams.

Maybe now?

Maybe when?

   We dare no longer pause.

We've evolved to reach this thinker's ground.

We the door-space clutter have brushed aside.

We grasped an eternal thought from the Universal
   Dream.

We are poised.

We are ready.

   No thing is left, behind which to hide.

No need to hide. No need for self-flagellation.

No object can your great journey disallow.

No well-meaning docent can alter your self-drawn
  dream.

No past to impair!

No future to ensnare!

  We live in the eternity of the now.

We have knelt before the Door in veneration of it.

We now peer through the keyhole, long occluded.

We see the marvelous, greater than our diminutive
  dreams.

We awe.

We sigh.

  So long deluded!

So, we're astonished when we push open the Door.

So easily it swings aside. No lock, a key to require.

So now we comprehend the puzzles of our dreams.

So, "keyhole" was an outline,

So that a window could exist,

  Our search to inspire.

Our search took on a greater intuition.

Our sight is not horizon-hindered, myopic seeing.

Our life is in the profusion of the Infinite's Dream.

Our hope is no wish.

Our task is no duty.

    There's no toil in simply *be ~ing.*

There's no otherworld deity our pledge to extort.

There's no sorcerer, our oath to implore.

There's no seer needed to reason this dream.

There's no dogma to abuse us.

There's no heresy to accuse us

    Here beyond the mythic Door.

Here is a place only seekers will find.

Here inside the Great Room is possibility.

Here is the locus of knowing, whether intuition or
    dream.

Here is richness of *be ~ing.*

Here is clarity of mind.

    This we now can see:

This present existence is an immortal's quest.

This quest is for the self's release, reborn.

This freedom nourishes the Infinite's Dream.

This Dream is to be lived.

This living is the Infinite's Life,

    The Infinite's Life in "our" form.

The Source

In the light of that solar disc called sun,
the invisible streams of energy come
as the flow of Life to enrich and caress
the many expressions of Its visibleness.

In the veil of risen vapors called clouds,
this flow of energy still abounds
in a gentle manner for tender born
of the ample expressions in Life's form.

In the spill of cleansing grace called rain,
the vapored energy is returned again
in a redemptive act of authentic ablution,
in the unguent guise of Life in solution.

In the want of that solar source called night,
the channel of energy is in abstracted light,
in the lunar reflection of a sun unknown
and the radiant heat of a day-warmed stone.

In this expense of energy given called "being,"
the invisible vitality is colored to be seen
in the visible beauty and expanse of nature,
in life-affirming words and deeds that nurture.

In this theatre of "being" called Life,
strength is given in the radiance of Its light,
in the nocturnal baptism, in the cleansing rain,
for Life gives always to all and each the same.

The Revel in Life

Life is like a voyage on a shoreless sea
with a destiny imagined with intention.
Amidst this passage comes revel of being
as we see when there seems no vision.

Though piloting this pathless sea alone,
with doldrums or storms fierce blown,
amidst all we're not adrift in life's revelry,
conscious the ship's course is known.

The sole keeper of day's invisible light,
the sun, shines warm and sensually bright.
Amidst this brilliant revel of sun's day,
where, that fleeting thought of night?

But the celestial circle is timely traced
and that keeper of light perfectly paced.
Amidst the color-laced revel of sunset,
alas, that fleeting thought is faced!

The navigator drafts the night course on.
The sky-lantern hangs until dawn.
Amidst this moon revel on dark tides,
see, that lesser light is not alone!

True, our sun is by day radiantly bright,
and stars, those twinkles of light
above and amidst our night revel,
are great suns also, just farther in sight.

Sun-stars near or far in a fixed position
become reference points of configuration,
and amidst this revel of keen vision
there is sight in this night navigation.

To us is given the compass and charts,
that lesser lantern and configured stars.
Amidst this night revel in pathless seas,
a confidence, a knowing indwells our hearts.

What say you of a new day's dawn
with the lesser light and stellar sight gone?
Amidst the sunray revel of a new morn
the true heart beams, a celestial glow born.

We speak the word that charts the way,
be it easier done in a bright sun day
or amidst night revel, pitched or waved.
See! The helmsman his true course has stayed!

And so on this journey in Earth's domain
with each night charted knowledge we gain,
amidst day's revelry as well with sun's blaze.
Behold! We see day and night the same!

A Stone in the Streambed

I

Tumbled from the mountainside
Stones rest in a streambed.
Insignificant in apparent size,
Stones fill this streambed.

Polished smooth with no harsh edge,
Rounded as time moved them along.
Insignificant in a giant's eyes,
In the streambed, this small stone.

Beneath the round edges and shine
Is the same pith as in the mount.
Significant to a boy's eyes,
In the streambed a stone is found.

II

His cause was to a warrior's field.
At the streambed he paused on his way.
Insignificant with no spear or armor,
A shepherd boy must wait.

Cast aside was warrior armor so large,
But shepherding had forged defensive ways.
Insignificant, they said, he plays a harp.
A shepherd boy at the streambed waits.

Beneath the youthful face and lean frame
Is the same pith as in the warrior.
Significant now, the slingshot he fingers.
He is more than a sheepherder.

III

A "so-called" giant appears on the crest,
Plundering his way from a mythic land.
Insignificant to the searching boy
Who picks a stone, the sling in hand.

Was it only a giant when up on the crest?
Did fear give it stature and fame?
Insignificant in warrior mind, the giant is faced
As the stone and sling take aim.

To the forehead the stone's mark
And soon among pebbles the mythic one lay.
Significant to all who face giants,
A stone in the streambed awaits.

IV

The mountain to the giant relates a truth,
As does the pebble to the giant slayer.
Insignificant that the mountain could crush a giant
With a quaking movement of an Earth layer.

The youth did not move the mountain
But a particle proved a solution:
Insignificant is the giant's incursion
When eyes behold truth and not illusion.

The pebble-stone, as part of the mountain,
Contained the same strata of latent power.
Significant, little truths fused to an adept hand
Contain all the might of the mountain tower.

V

The shepherd boy to the warrior relays insight,
As does the pebble-stone to the mountain's height:
Significant that an appearance of greatness
Does not suspend a lesser one's might.

The defeated warriors finished warrior training,
But the specious goliath knew no battle schools.
Significant that this untrained shepherd boy
Triumphed, not knowing the battle rules.

Guarding his flock he won battles with lions.
With meditating harp, in awareness he's led.
Significant, when the "so-called" giants arise,
That mountain-stone is in your streambed.

One

Two hands one task
Two feet only one path
Two eyes but single sight
There's only one heart

1.

Two hands but only one task,
Be it the tiny hand to clasp
Or a gripless hand to grasp,
To lend them cheerfully when asked.

Hands that comfort when hearts are broken
And hands that sign, no word spoken.
The extended hand, vulnerable, open,
The heart's true symbol, no greater token.

The open hand your spirit frees.
An outstretched hand life's gift receives.
But capable hands lifeless freeze
When fingers curl, by anger seized.

Self-Inflicted Nonsense and lack.
Who tied your hands behind your back?
Free the two to do one task,
One hand to receive and one to give back.

Hands clapped for joy, a hand to hold,
Warm hands for the hand that's cold,
Things just to touch, things meant to grasp.
Two hands but only one task.

2.
Two feet only one path,
Be it a high road, a garden path,
The low road, the beaten path,
A rut, a maze, a labyrinth;

Or mountain trail, an esplanade,
Obstacle course, a promenade,
A catwalk, a gangplank, a racetrack,
A detour, a cliffside, a switchback!

Find a dance step, a telling song,
Another pilgrim walking alone,
A cooling brook to rest along
And note another milestone.

Choosing a path in servile deference
Leaving all to circuitous chance
May lead to elongated distance,
Pacing a circle's circumference.

Footprints are temporal and cannot last.
Tarrying there is not life's task
And when the horizon at last is met,
'Twas only one path wherever it led.

3.

Two eyes but single sight,
May be dimmed with dusk-drawn light
Or blinded by conflagration bright,
Or non-visual in darkest night.

With inner sight to our path we're led,
No longer to wander a vagabond tread.
By inner sight life essence is fed
Making true what's thought and said.

When what is seen tends displeasure
Change the rule used as measure.
Opt for insight and not censure.
Change the view to change your nature.

Be the eyes for the traveler blind,
Eyes that are shared, his path to find.
When the sight-pools sparkle and shine
They mirror the lofty, the sublime.

The windows of the soul, it's said,
Where truth is told and read.
The path of the soul radiates incarnate light
When the journeyer travels with single sight.

4.

Be inclusive of all, there's only one heart.
Of cultures there are many with customs apart.
Finding common ground not caustic retort
Makes differences smaller, enlarging the heart.

There's more than one road, more than one choice.
There's more than one vision, more than one voice.
There's more than one emotion, choose to rejoice.
Exercise as a gift that privilege of choice.

There are different skins, different hair
And differing words but the same prayer.
It's the same sun upon all to share
And all breath is of the one and same air.

An open mind stretches wide the vision
And this peripheral sight gives depth, realism.
The individual with the universal sees no schism.
Life magically reveals as light through a prism.

The heart as an icon is the center of being,
A symbol of love and care unending.
An open mind is the place of beginning,
Then with one heart comes true seeing.

5.

So let your feet feel your path.
Let your hands be guided to task.
Intend with heart to seeing aright
And hold that vision with single sight.

Earth and sun and myriad stars,
Planets and moons and meteors
Moving and circling, eclipsing some.
The *uni*verse is still one.

Celebrations, chanters, and canticles,
Incense, oblations, and candles.
We sense it, say it. Do we see it?
There is only one spirit.

It's in the beauty of the newly born.
It's in the wisdom of the aged and timeworn.
It's the same smile on another face.
There is only one human race.

Be it continent, island, any hemisphere,
This latitude, that longitude, there or here,
The *uni*verse has placed you true
Simply because there's only one you.

Book of Laughter and Logic

"I think I'm losing my mind."

True Confessions (and False)

"I'm living with my nose to the grindstone.
I'm working my fingers to the bone.
They're eating us out of house and home.
I think I'm losing my mind."

1. "I'm living with my nose to the grindstone."

What? Living with the nose to the stone?
Have you ever seen a stone-ground nose?
If the nose is to the stone that close
Then eyes are crossed and focus is gone.

I declare,
Lifting the head and seeing aright
The aggrieving grindstone
Drops from sight.

2. *"I'm working my fingers to the bone."*

What? Working the fingers to the bone?
If seeing a bare, bloody, finger bone, take heed.
Nearby could be a very messy deed,
For when mind is inactive, blind fingers work alone.

I declare,
Dropping busy doings and engaging mind
Engenders greater deeds
Of a much cleaner kind.

3. *"They're eating us out of house and home."*

What? Eating away at house and home?
Can you imagine such a diet,
Or even possible someone would try it?
What if you fed them more than house alone?

I declare,
a nutritional regimen of love and caring
Will grow the kids,
The house sparing.

4. *"I think I'm losing my mind."*

What? Think of losing the cat, but the mind?
Can you see a sign posted in this regard:
    'Lost - One Tabby Mind. Reward'
And what to do if this is your find?

I declare,
If constructive thinking you choose,
Then muddled mental clutter
Is all you'll lose.

roll the dice

in the dark of the night
in a wee little hour
at times in such fright
a horror with such power
oft taking macabre shape
a changeling form
you cannot escape
what fear what alarm

in the dark of the night
in a wee little hour
comes a wonder in sight
a magical power
like a bird on the wing
which changes form
now it's you on the wind
no fear no alarm

once again comes the night . . .

who designed this scheme
realistic fright
or
fantasy dream

Who Wrote the Book

Who wrote the book you read?
In what tongue was it written?
How many times has it been translated?
From how many languages originated?
How much could be fantasy or mythological?
Who wrote this book?

Who wrote the book you read?
Is it as a novel written?
Are hero and antagonist related?
Has true authorship been shown?
Is this fiction a story believable?
Who wrote this book?

Who wrote the book you read?
Is it as poetry written?
Was its rhetoric to staccato transmuted?
Whose authority concurred?
Are its verses coherently logical?
Who wrote this book?

Who wrote the book you read?
Is it as biography written?
Is author and subject objectively one?
Do reader and subject appear connected?
Does the subject emerge knowable?
Who wrote this book?

Do you know who writes the book?
As autobiography it is being written.
Will its foibles be seen and deciphered?
Will the agent of these discern none?
Is this writing hand truly invincible?
Guess who's writing the book you read.

What if We Never Left the Garden

What if we never left the Garden?
What if Eden still flourishes?
What if Creator is yet abiding
with a voice that ever nourishes?
Why then are we still in hiding?
What if we never left the Garden?

I

Suppose the First Man never left Eden.
What if there never was a deception,
and "evil" was only a pretense
that exists in misguided perception?
What if believing Creator is ever in absence
brings into life this mistaken conception?

II

What if Eden still flourishes?
Suppose there is no "forbidden tree."
Is innocence just reason's absence,

the loss of which makes one flee?
What if Creator is still in presence
and healing is in every tree?

III

Suppose Creator is here still,
as Life Force, all creation inclusive.
Did the informer give the wrong news
and Creator is never elusive?
What if the scribes tended myopic views
and Creator is never exclusive?

IV

Perhaps the perennial voice is not audible
because we've cultured a deafened ear.
What if we've formed the wrong conclusion?
Could we listen in a different sphere,
one not based on fear and illusion?
What if the Garden is still here?

V

Why then are we crouched in hiding?
Where could we possibly go?
To cloud-shrouded peak or pit of fear?
Is there any place Creator doesn't know?
Is there any place other than here,
be it scaled heights or depths below?

VI

Suppose then to our missteps and more
we spoke gracious words of pardon.
It is then the Soul hears Creator's voice,
and sensing this, spirits enhearten.
Let us emerge from our hiding choice
to see we've never left the Garden.

The Greatest Reward

I

Some say, "Seeing is believing,"
And *Others* are swayed to believe it so.
They don't see that some achieving
Can rival a magician's show.

Some act like believing is seeing
While *Others* confirm and are prone to fright.
They don't know that negative believing
Can conjure a hostile sight.

Some at times experience seeing aright
But *Others* offend this new achieving.
They don't see that mind-eye's sight
Can reveal a greater *see ~ing*.

II

We sometimes say, "It can't be done,"
And *Others* agree to impossibility.
We need to see that sight alone
May pose a slight disability.

We sometimes act when *We* haven't "seen"
And *Others* attest *Our* deeds delinquent.
We need to see that what could have been
May still be *Our* able achievement.

We sometimes experience *do* ~*ing* with "sight"
And *Others* benefit from *Our* succeeding.
Can *We* see then, in this new light,
A wondrous state of *be* ~*ing?*

III

Once, *Some* could the vision easily sway,
Others could dim and cloud this *see ~ing.*
Now giving attention to life in this way
Renews that intent to simply *be ~ing.*

Once *I* acted from group-mind as *We*
And with *Others* resolved what *We* did.
Now the heart's desire to "Be"
Gives gracious birth to every deed.

So once experiencing this art of *be ~ing*
And from the *Others* made free,
Each thought, word, and action bring
New and wondrous things to be.

IV

The religionist looks to a god outside,
With obeisance and hope, no certainty,
When all that's needed is known deep inside:
Be ~ing is a great reality.

When the mind's eye is privileged to sight
And the doings are freed from group-guessing,
There comes a truth like a ray of light:
Be ~ing is the greatest blessing.

The true soul is then able to view
Assets, renown or other acquired,
And all that's seen can't equal this truth:
Be ~ing is the greatest reward.

Why Beauty is Missing

I

When searching for enriching themes
in this weighted world, this pallid state,
with no inspiration in its sullied schemes,
pause your quest and contemplate:

Can the vacant canvas refuse the brush?
Does the moist clay rebuff the wheel?
Can the loom resist both warp and weft?
Can the stone deny chisel-steel?

Can the paper reject the pen?
Does the flute to breath have choice?
Can the harp simply forbid the touch?
Can the song abhor and repress the voice?

II

How interesting this predicament!
In this absent splendored state what is amiss?
The repressed participation significant
as you pause and consider this:

Is the painter avoiding the canvas?
To the potter is the clay unknown?
Has the weaver idled the loom,
the sculptors scorned the stone?

Could the poet ignore the pen,
and the breath rebuff the flute?
Are the fingers spurning the harp,
the song silenced by voices mute?

III

Now the clues to this beauteous state
or reasons for absence or its demise
seem to surface and challenge the stalemate.
With inspiration and insight we realize:

Intent with effort imprints the blank canvas,
and kneads a new form of the clay.
We fashion fabric, threading the loom.
Enthused, we in stone a likeness shape.

The poet inspired pens wonders in words,
our touch of strings brings melody and tone.
The life-breath applied enchants the flute.
Now, the universal voice gives wing to song.

~~Today's~~ Life's Lesson
by Prof. Ratio Cognoscendi

Listen as though you are being told a great story.

Speak as though you are reading a great book aloud.

Sit like you are a stack of silver coin.

Walk as if each step is counted by all those around.

Stand as if you are the tallest tree in the wood.

Let your eyes be open for wonders.

Let your thoughts come . . . and go.

Let beneficent ideas find their mental space.

Let your mind know that you are in control.

Let your words to the world be as a medicant.

Let your speech to yourself be ever affirming.

To Students:

1) Note the absence of *Don'ts* as they lack quality and hinder good character with overuse

2) Note the lesson is an endorsement to *Do*, and this allows for the *Let-ing* that follows

3) See the professor's name in *Webster's Third New International Dictionary*

Magnificentia

Standing bold as the granite dome
Metamorphic splendor or a marble wall
Marching peaks or sentinels alone
Magnificent mountains, one and all.

Standing solitaire or among many numbered
Stately poised in lesser height or tall
Lavishly cloaked or scarcely encumbered
Magnificent trees, one and all.

Standing to light and loving the land
Cheerful and small or noble and tall
Shouting hues from the rainbow band
Magnificent flowers, one and all.

Standing alone or group-membered
Giant-sized or relatedly small
Continent ranging or one-spot anchored
Magnificent creatures, one and all.

Standing out in darkest night
Close and large or distantly small
In cosmic hiding or pulsing bright
Magnificent stars, one and all.

Standing true each preceding line
When read again see to recall
Mirrored in nature and cosmos we find
Magnificent us, one and all.

CODA:
Standing bold as the granite dome
Diverse splendor or a sculpted wall
Parading pinnacles or watchmen alone
Magnificent us, like mountains all.

Standing solitaire or among many numbered
Regally graceful slight or tall
Abundantly clothed or barely encumbered
Magnificent us, like trees all.

Standing to light and loving the land
Radiant and slight or brilliant and tall
Expressing hues like a prism band
Magnificent us, like flowers all.

Established alone or communal numbered
Towering tall or comparatively small
Continent reaching or locally anchored
Magnificent us, like the created all.

Standing out in the faintest light
Close and sizeable or distance small
Plain-sight hiding or near in sight
Magnificent us, like the stars all.

Standing true line by line
When read with insight we recall
Mirrored in nature and cosmos we find
Magnificent us, one and all.

Book of Memory's Gallery

"... it stood solidly anchored to bayou land."

A Different Kind of Cowboy

He stood a wrangler at twenty
But not out on the lone prairie.
No howling by coyotes here,
It's mosquitoes buzzing each ear.
No longhorns or whiteface his care,
It's brahma facing bugs and salt air.

When he was born among wrangler folks
Who lived on a *chenier* amid the oaks,
His grandfather planted a seedling tree
Near the bayou, called *d'Acadie*,
Beside the corral and watering tank,
A clamshell's throw from bayou bank.

At seven that sturdy lad you'd see
Is the norm on *Bayou d'Acadie*.
No struggle for health or good food here.
There's beef and boar, wild duck, marsh deer,
A barnyard of fowl and seafood to catch.
There's a smokehouse full and a garden patch.

When he was ten, chores were his.
No shortcuts to hanker, no milking to miss.
The cow was half-brahma so don't take a seat,
Hold that milk pail and watch her feet.
Eye the tail switch, cocklebur thick,
Don't get tangled in a sideways kick.

When he was twelve, the winter was harsh
With a hoary frost whitening the marsh.
It was short-lived as the geese flew north
Calling for the return of summer's warmth.
The heat did arrive, moisture in tow,
Carried on clouds from the Gulf of Mexico.

When a teen the chores were no more
For now it was work, more than before.
Herd through the chute and vaccinate,
Roundup and brand, work until late.
Between frequent rains bale hay,
That's after noon in the heat of the day.

In his twenties the big hurricane blew.
The marsh herd loss was more than a few
'Cause the great wind pushed a mighty tide
That took too many days to subside.
With the high water came gators and snakes
From ravaged *cheniers* and flattened canebrakes.

At thirty the new cattle-trucks arrive,
Putting an historical end to the cattle drive
That moved the wintered herd from marsh,
A swim of two bayous while heading north
To a summer of prairie meadow to graze.
The 'drive' now took hours, not days.

In his forties there came great change.
Still had mosquitoes but no open range.
Fenced-off roads, barbed wire stretched,
High levees made, a deeper ditch.
All meant for good, progress it's named
But wrangling here was forever changed.

Now he is older, that's what he'd say,
Older and wiser, forlorn in a way.
He'll tell of high tides and hurricanes,
Catching the last of De Soto's mustangs,
Being pinned by the horns of a bull,
And knowing which heifer to cull.

Now he's wiser in life's living
And always ready with advice-giving.
Days are filled with worth indeed
Sowing his wisdom like scattering seed,
Gator-torn fish nets mending
And gall-darn weeds attending.

Look for him down the bayou if you go.
Ask old-timer or youngster, they'll know
Where you'll find this different cowpoke.
His grandfather's seedling is that great oak
Where *Bayou d'Acadie* bends to the west.
If he's not around, that's where he's laid to rest.

Gone from the Bayou
c'est comme ceci– it's like this

Gone from the bayou but the bayou isn't gone.
It flows in my veins, fontal and fervid flows,
carrying in its magic embrace as it goes,
my mystery, that life I call my own.

Gone from the maison but the maison isn't gone.
It houses my heart strongly, encases
it sturdily as it embraces
my mystery, that life I call my own.

Gone from the ancestors' home but they aren't gone.
They live in my dreams, magically live,
enriching, encoding, revealing what they give
to the mystery, that life I call my own.

Gone from the past but is the past gone?
It's similarly afar and suspiciously near,
awakening insight or mustering fear.
What mystery that life I call my own!

le bayou
Gone from the bayou but *le bayou* isn't gone.
It flows in my arteries and puddles in my tears,
nourishing fates and washing away fears,
cradling me gently as its own.

It flows in my veins like a life-blood,
like it was to the ancestors a sustenance source
or for the *pirogue* or a houseboat, the watercourse,
flowing steady in spring and fall, drought and flood.

Carried in its surreal embrace as a mystery
that to an outsider musters fright
but to its own a riddle of solace and delight.
To its begotten it's both now and history.

My own mystery animates sinew and bone.
A mystery cannot be framed in black and white
nor can it be materialized for touch or sight.
Gone from the bayou but *le bayou* isn't gone.

la maison
Gone from the maison but *la maison* isn't gone.
It cannot be found along the bayou streams
but summarily appears in bayou dreams,
as in my life the maison lives on.

It houses my heart in a castle-like stand
though single-wall cypress boarded its frame,
and in hurricanes and winds or storms and rain
it stood solidly anchored to bayou land.

Holding it sturdily with heart and soul inside,
this wondrous wattle of flesh and bone
embraces that which is me alone
as a new maison for the life to abide.

My own mystery as the maison has shown
makes entreaty to a nobler life to live
and knowledge of a greater gift to give.
Gone from the maison but *la maison* isn't gone.

les ancetres

Gone from the ancestors' home but they aren't gone.
They're living in the codes on a spiral arranged
from retiring cells to embryonic exchanged,
mixing the mystery that becomes mine alone.

They live in my dreams not just my history,
deftly choosing at what unpredictable hour
to visit the dreamtime with subliminal power,
influencing what is me and coddling the mystery.

Enriching and encoding or prompting and revealing,
entrancingly real *les ancetres* come calling.
Mysterious at times but likewise enthralling,
bending the ordinary and subtleties concealing.

My own mystery owes homage to ancestors gone.
Encoding is gifted but I may choose
to evolve and transcend and comprehend the clues
to my mystery, that life I call my own.

le passé
Moved on from the past and *le passé* is gone.
It levitates in memory and may momentarily appear
trying the present to ensnare and drag arrear
to mystify that life I call my own.

So it is here in this patent moment alone
living in the present not what's coming or was last
but rather gaining the future and redeeming the past,
building the mystery I call my own.

Living on the bayou this mystery was shown
but life has no choice geographical space.
Living true makes each stead a special place
where the mystery of life and breath are known.

Gone from *le bayou* and *la petite maison*,
from the home of *les ancetres* on bayou streams.
Le bayou is my blood. *Les ancetres* draft my dreams
and *la maison* cradles this life I call my own.
c'est comme ça -
it's like that

Lizabette

She was born on the *chenier* bordering
Screaming Eagle stream, where it flows
in the shadow of a great mound of shell.
In this lowland only the oak could match
the mound's height, the mound there always,
says a Great-One's tale.

This was the child of a maiden girl whose family
journeyed to a distant ranch, spurning barriers
to such overlong travel.
The bayou lands held no secrets to mound people
who lived there, because food and shelter
outweighed storms and peril.

This father was a good horseman, for his people
had mustangs descended from the Spanish horses
of De Soto and his kind.
These horses thrived after being abandoned
when these fortune hunters lost their way,
their health and mind.

In this new home the maiden learned to ride
though given few chances due her status
and lean years.
The rancher's young son taught her and won
her trust. Youth and fervor prevailed
and love cancelled all fears.

Though only teens they had a child, a girl
loved by all, but the ranch owner objected
upon identity of the father.
Back to the *chenier* the family moved,
the boy objecting to this hardship
and somehow hoping to follow.

His desire was not to be and his child was taken
to live as her maiden mother had
with the great mound near.
The mother learned French, now the language of
trade between arriving settlers
and people of the *chenier.*

Sadly, her mother died leaving the family forlorn.
Aback the mustang with dog at her side
she rode the *chenier* alone.
Words of sadness found her father, one she had
barely known and he arrived at the mound of shell
with hope to take her home.

The Great-Ones persuaded her to journey
with her father, taking her deer-hunting dog
and mustang on this trail.
She was met by unknown family, understanding and
loving, and here were younger siblings, more family
than at the mound of shell.

There were non-mustang horses and brahma
cattle that would survive the heat and prosper
the people living here.
New experiences abounded. An American boy was
there but there was no mound of shell like that
on her mother's *chenier.*

The two taught the dog to work, giving commands
to heel or to head, and found others in ranches near
like her glass-eyed leopard hound.
Away many years from the *chenier* she soon forgot
her mother's tongue becoming so French in speech
and ways none dare recall shell mound.

The government census takers asked how she
in teen years now, was not counted ten years earlier.
No answers to be found.
Perhaps her father thought it wise to stay apart
from the past. Did the child of the shell maiden
ever visit the shell mound?

Years went by with marriage and family,
nine children arrived, the bayou land now crowded
due a peaceful site here found.
The wrangler boy she'd married spoke English
and she French, in a grand Cajun cottage
far from the shell mound.

The shell mound was devoured by a machine with
great bites, and spread over muddy trails,
easing travel for those from outside.
What labor and years were required for a mound
as tall as the oaks! How easy it was to flatten
and the mound did subside.

A skeleton was unearthed from its shell-white rest
there and displayed in a doctor's office
where so few gave it pause.
Word spread of the mound girl's past, tongues
spitefully whispering, speaking of mother
and daughter as "old Indians and squaws."

Was there some untold reason why we brought food
and clothing to a native group living in cabins with
earthen floors?
When asked often of French-speaking aunts for
answers, nothing was shared but blank expressions,
vacant stares like closed doors.

I hope this child of shell maiden remembered
the shell mound and sounds of the Great-Ones'
tongue though many years gone.
She did recall the swamp herbs and each visit
shared their use. If no one seemed interested
she hunted the lowland alone.

Years later at a daughter's passing, ancestor's names
were read aloud, the French Acadian names
prevalent, going back to tenth generation.
Semaire, Savoie, Moreau, LeFleur,
Melanson, Marcantel, Francoise, de la Fosse,
Olivier, Miller and more to mention.

How beautiful to hear them read, and through
the solemnity, smiles. With few French speakers
left, a heavier sadness was present there.
But the ancestors of this one's mother had no
mention. Who were her Great-Ones? Why can't we
call for their presence here?

Lizabette.

Her name was alone.

She was my grandmother,

Great-Mother to some.

She lived in years a century plus one.

Lizabette,

Great-Mother,

Grandmother to some,

This remembrance is for you.

May it be read for a century plus one.

In Memory's Gallery
Ode to Gregory

The tired cottage posed at a tilt,
its wood weathered and pale.
The tattered shutters hung in a wilt,
the roofline sagging and frail.

A room inside was suffocating and stale,
the static air cloying, damp and heady.
The light was smothered by an unseen veil,
the once colorful rugs bare and thready.

She wore a sallow dress definitely old,
a bit frayed from use and well worn
with age hiding in each crease and fold
giving it image both familiar and forlorn.

As I scan this canvas behind shuttered eyes
I'm caught in a space both cloudy and clear.
Searching with diligence the scenes that arise
there's the tiniest tug at the past here.

Is this that state betwixt waking and sleeping
where between worlds you're privileged to be?
Things familiar, taken from memory's keeping,
are given new life, the implausible to see.

A pale blue ribbon tied her hair now thin,
its whiteness yellowed by languishing lamplight.
The wrinkled lips parted for a sly grin,
her deep-set eyes were telling and bright.

"Welcome to Memory's Gallery," she whispered,
and I drew closer, every word to understand.
"Come, come. I've been waiting." She gestured
with motion of a pale pink hand.

The closeness seemed a magical space,
its ambiance with a faint fragrance sewn,
a delicate scent I could not name or place.
To an enchantment I seemed to be drawn.

Into the clear, watery eyes I drifted
and into those mystical pools I fell.
Then a delicate younger hand was lifted
to steady my step, my alarm to quell.

With the return of self-composure and relief
the scene has shifted and somehow changed.
The Enchantress had morphed beyond belief.
Was this perceptual or essentially arranged?

Her soothing voice was mellow and clear,
her lips lightly colored and lush.
A bright blue ribbon held her curly hair,
her radiance enhanced with a faint blush.

Her dress had delicate crisp lace,
its whiteness captured in the window light,
mutely illuminating her radiant face
and giving her eyes a far deeper sight.

The hand that had before steadied me
now motioned another view to access.
The Enchantress then readied me
for a broader vision to possess.

Looking again at the old cottage I'd seen
I was amazed by all I viewed.
Its lines were now straight and clean,
its semblance and state, vivid and renewed.

The rooms were quite airy and bright.
It seemed all furnishings were new.
Windows were open to breeze and light.
Gentle voices were heard. Laughter, too.

"This is Memory's Gallery," she purred.
I was close enough to understand.
"You've been waiting to see." I concurred.
She moved close enough to take my hand.

I saw her gaze was past me.
When I turned I was in a great hall.
The room had expanded to be a gallery
with life-sized pictures along the wall.

I was drawn to the first one quite near
and what I saw was not anticipated
though what I expected was not quite clear.
There was life and sound, its scenes animated.

A gentle breeze pushed at the window drapes.
Is this the room I saw before?
Now, what sweetness a lullaby makes
as a child plays on a rug-covered floor.

The scenes changed with years going by
as the Enchantress led on, being guide.
The child, older now, had begun to cry.
I wanted to rush to his side.

We moved along and he is older now,
busy with schoolmate and friend.
The scenes were at times familiar somehow
but time and space would not blend.

Now a young man in the next gallery frame,
his love is painting, his passion is art.
At the following scene my lips form a name.
My heart races. The dream falls apart.

Copied from the past, the tragedy I see again
and feel the emotions from down deep arise.
My breath comes in gasps and escapes in pain.
Somewhere I hear loved ones' cries.

I relive the moments from beginning to ending,
from the first news to the choking silent grief,
from denial to acceptance, heart-rending,
challenging every skein of belief.

The gallery air thickens. I want to flee.
I feel alone. Where is my guide?
From out of the teary fog she reached for me
and my heart was steadied. Anxieties subside.

"There's one more scene," she said.
I was more than reluctant to go.
With a smile she added, "Are you willing to be led?
You will find what you've waited to know."

When I gave her my now steadied hand
it seemed we had only turned around,
and there in front of the final frame we stand
with recall of a familiar scene and sound.

I searched every detail to note and retain
as the tragic youth stood before me tall.
I asked, "What happened? Please explain."
His quick description had no cloud or pall.

With no prompt or wait, a response came:
"Oh, Dad, it's a miracle that's happened, you
    know."
He said it matter-of-fact. I accepted the same.
Around his image moved an effervescent glow.

There was no need or desire to linger,
to dwell on each vivid and telling act.
He pointed to his watch with art-stained finger
and flashed a smile to which I did react.

The face was his, the hair, the speech,
but something about his eyes startled me so
as he moved closer, within my reach.
He said he couldn't be late. He must go.

"I'm on my way to an orientation,
and Language 101," he sighs,
flashing his unique facial expression,
one I knew despite the startling eyes.

Then he walked past me on my right.
I was still mesmerized by those eyes.
I knew he was walking forever out of sight.
I couldn't turn for saying good-byes.

My heavy feet seemed glued in place.
Not that leaving was my desire.
I felt I was standing in sacred space.
How could anything else so raptly inspire?

Then I felt a gentle hand, a soft impress
from behind me, the direction he had gone.
She stepped to the fore, the Enchantress,
this docent to all that was shown.

"Who are you?" I asked in tender speech
for it seemed a close camaraderie.
In unsteady moments she had been within reach
her voice, her touch, great strengths to me.

"I am Memory," she replied, each word distinct.
"I am keeper of the Past, of all that transpired,
whether proffered by intuition or instinct,
whether common and familiar or tragic and
    conspired.

"I am Guardian of the Soul, that eternal flame
which cannot know hurt, harm or pain,
loss or degradation, deceit or blame.
It is all-consuming of earthly gain.

"It is the Law of the Universe at work here.
The struggle and suffering are for the finite alone.
That which is Eternal is not wrought with fear,
for fear keeps the Infinite unknown."

The Enchantress moved near, my hand to grasp.
Reveling in closeness, I saw her eyes once more
and those deep pools of blue triggered a gasp.
The same startling eyes as the tragic one before!

She loosed each hand with a light squeeze
and her fingers did gently my eyelids close.
"There's more for you to understand," she said.
"More of the timeless, the infinite to disclose.

"Memory's Gallery can be blindly visited
when another 'you' tells each scene descriptively
and each frame is mentally formed and posed,
but fails to reveal what the Soul must see.

"To live and re-live memories by this demand
diminishes the wealth of truths to be known.
Ask for a guide, a docent, a steady hand
so unblinded eyes can deeper knowledge be
        shown."

The last lines seemed to come from behind me,
and as I opened my eyes and turned around
I was surprised in what I came to see:
the Enchantress now aged in person and gown.

The room, the rug, the house and door,
I saw the same timeworn frame
that had gently pulled me in before
to enliven the past from which it came.

Resisting the pull of the deep blue eyes
that anchored the enchanted face,
I managed to feel with several tries
moored again in present time and space.

My waking now was sentient, a rosy glow
from the setting sun invading the window bar.
How much time elapsed I could not know
but Sun's shadows had not traveled far.

I was conscious of a warmth, a glow inside,
echoing the luminous aura of the space.
On impulse I audibly thanked my guide
and allowed a broad smile to caress my face.

Memory would certainly return again
when the mind visited that gallery of recall.
There would be new insights to attain
if I summon a guide to Memory's hall.

Elegy for Greg

Among the woods
These sylvan whispers
Earthen ashes lie
Giving the clouds
Those risen vapors
His spirit to fly

Two seeds were planted in the garden of my heart.
They grew side by side and became two trees.
Two trees were growing in the garden of my heart.
They grew side by side but were two different trees.

Different trees, equally loved, no longer grow there.
They grew side by side but only one remains.
One tree is growing now in the garden of my heart.
The other is gone. Raw earth is there now.

One tree spreads over the garden of my heart.
Will it cover the chasm where the young tree stood?
Many tears have fallen because that tree is gone.
But none have fallen on the raw earth there.

Are those tears to nurture that newly planted tree
In another garden, the Garden Beyond?
Is the sorrow that rises from the depths of my being
Helping that new garden grow?

Then let the tears flow, and let the sorrows rise,
For one day I'll see the Garden Beyond
And I'll recognize the seedling that came
From the garden of my heart.

The Greg Totem Pole

The Greg Totem Pole was set as a memorial styled after the 'story poles' of the peoples living on the upper Pacific coast of North America. This is their creation tale that may be seen, not just told.

At the top of this eight-foot totem, Raven has captured the sun for mankind who has labored in the dark, never becoming accustomed to it. He inhabits the skies but is perched on the head of Bear. Bear captured the moon's reflection and brought it back to the earth dwellers.

Part of Raven's wing appears human-like with an arm and hand, but he has raven feet as he perches on Bear's head. Bear holds the moon with claws but he has human-like feet as he stands on Turtle's back. The people said that when there were no humans nearby, Raven took off his raven clothes and Bear took off his bear clothes, and they were actually people. Therefore, the animals were treated with respect as all of nature was one family.

Earth is represented by the turtle on which Bear stands, a great turtle floating on the great seas. The fish near Turtle's head is an orca whale symbolizing the life of the oceans.

The small faces seen on Turtle's back, Bear's arm, and Raven's wing represent the "life force" present in all living things. Yes, there is "life force" even in the earth. At the top of this story pole is an upside down face representing the clouds and benevolent forces. They actually see things in the correct way. If you lie down on your back at the foot of the totem and look up at those faces, they will be smiling at you.

This story totem was commissioned by a private school in Los Angeles, California in 2002. It was carved by the author, painted in muted colors, and stands centered, overlooking the playground.

Afterword

Born in a bayou parish on Louisiana's gulf coast and raised on a ranch, many were my exposures to both earth and spirit. With languid cicada-serenaded afternoons amid moss-draped oaks, or the misty humid nights with a chorus of rain frogs (from the tubular unfurled banana leaves hugging the roofline between *gallerie* and *garconniere*), life was not at a loss in this mystical arena.

From this 'incubator' and a mother who cherished her monthly book-club selections, dropping all to read more than a few pages upon their arrival, I saw the beauty and lure of literature and poetry. I still recall the first book ordered for me about a near-sighted American bison.

Despite very few available details (except the 1900 census record) and closed-mouth elders, I became aware of my native heritage, and much more knowing of the fate of my other ancestry. No Cajun forgets *le Grand Dérangement* of 1755, when thousands of French Acadians were inhumanely loaded on ships by the new English governor, and forced into exile. Some of my ancestors were among the many who found their way to the French-speaking parishes of coastal Louisiana, prospering in this lush subtropical land.

Following the coastline a few hundred miles west and south, you will be in much the same topography. Here in the Mexican states of Veracruz and Tabasco is the birthplace of the oldest civilization in Mesoamerica, the Olmec. Into these great coastal nurseries of humankind and the varied cultures, I entered and became a seeker wanting to share some of the happenings along that path.

It is part of the record of these successive years, from a curiosity-filled childhood to the very present, where awe and wonder can still exist when looking at a 'world' within the world. Knowing that this fascinating symphony of sight, sound, and script must be shared, this collection of poetry evolved.

Glossary

Acadie Fr. (ah-kah-JEE) Acadia; name of New France colony on northeast coast of North America

bayou (BAH-yu or BAHy) from Choctaw *bayuk*; a slow moving stream in river deltas; as in down to the 'BAH-yu' or 'BAHy-dah-kah-jee' for Bayou d'Acadie

brahma a breed developed from Zebu cattle of India; with thick skin, large ears, and a shoulder hump; resistant to insects and extreme heat

Cajun descendants of Acadians; elided from the French *Acadien* (ah-kah-JAn) or just 'a Cajun'

canebrake a dense growth of giant cane

chenier Fr. (shin-YEAR) a wooded ridge or sandy hummock in marshlands of coastal Louisiana

cypress a deciduous conifer in lowlands; resistant to rot and insects; related to the redwood tree

DeSoto Spanish explorer in Louisiana in 1542

gall-darn a mild expletive for g**-damn

pirogue (pee-ROHG or PEE-rawg) from Carib *piragua*; a dugout canoe

Printed in the United States
By Bookmasters